.95

W9-BEE-226

DEC

The Nature and Science of
EGGS

Jane Burton and Kim Taylor

Gareth Stevens Publishing
MILWAUKEE

For a free color catalog describing Gareth Stevens Publishing's list of high-quality books
and multimedia programs, call 1-800-542-2595 (USA) or 1-800-461-9120 (Canada).
Gareth Stevens Publishing's Fax: (414) 225-0377.
See our catalog, too, on the World Wide Web: gsinc.com

Library of Congress Cataloging-in-Publication Data

Burton, Jane.
The nature and science of eggs / by Jane Burton and Kim Taylor.
p. cm. -- (Exploring the science of nature)
Includes bibliographical references and index.
Summary: Describes the purpose, parts, fertilization, development,
and other aspects of eggs. Includes experiments and activities.
ISBN 0-8368-2105-X (lib. bdg.)
1. Embryology--Juvenile literature. 2. Eggs--Juvenile literature.
[1. Eggs. 2. Embryology.] I. Taylor, Kim. II. Title.
III. Series: Burton, Jane. Exploring the science of nature.
QL956.5.B88 1998
591.4'68--dc21 98-6330

First published in North America in 1998 by
Gareth Stevens Publishing
1555 North RiverCenter Drive, Suite 201
Milwaukee, Wisconsin 53212 USA

This U.S. edition © 1998 by Gareth Stevens, Inc. Created with original © 1998 by
White Cottage Children's Books. Text and photographs © 1998 by Jane Burton and
Kim Taylor. The photographs on pages 12 (*above*) and 13 are by Mark Taylor. The
photograph on page 12 (*below*) is by Jan Taylor. Conceived, designed, and produced
by White Cottage Children's Books, 29 Lancaster Park, Richmond, Surrey
TW10 6AB, England. Additional end matter © 1998 by Gareth Stevens, Inc.

The rights of Jane Burton and Kim Taylor to be identified as the authors of this work
have been asserted by them in accordance with the Copyright, Design and Patents
Act 1988. Educational consultant, Jane Weaver; scientific adviser, Dr. Jan Taylor.

Printed in the United States of America

1 2 3 4 5 6 7 8 9 02 01 00 99 98

Contents

Words that appear in the glossary are printed in **boldface** type the first time they occur in the text.

The Purpose of Eggs

Which came first, the chicken or the egg? This is a question known as a **conundrum**, for which there is supposed to be no answer. The truth, however, is that the egg came first. Animals laid eggs millions of years before chickens ever appeared in the world. Chicken ancestors were probably laying eggs that looked like chicken eggs long before they **evolved** into chickens.

Eggs have existed for a very long time. Before there were eggs, animals **reproduced** by budding. Sea anemones and some other simple animals still do this. For an active animal, however, a bud growing out of its side would be bothersome. By laying eggs, some animals produce thousands of offspring with very little trouble.

Eggs grow inside a female animal. Once the eggs have been laid, the female is usually free to move around without them. Each egg is an amazing structure. An egg appears simple, but it contains all the materials and information needed to start a new animal life.

Opposite: Chickens lay eggs. Eggs hatch into chicks **(top)**. Chicks grow into chickens. But which came first, chickens or eggs?

Below: This illustration shows a baby dinosaur hatching from an egg millions of years ago.

Below: This sea anemone produces eggs as well as buds.

Below: All birds lay eggs, and many build complicated nests for the eggs. This nest and eggs belong to a bullfinch.

Egg Shapes

Top: An ostrich's egg is the largest egg of any bird alive today. It can weigh over 3 pounds (1.5 kilograms).

If you look at a bird's egg from the end, it appears round. This is because eggs are formed in a round tube called the **oviduct** inside a female bird's body. Viewed from other directions, bird eggs appear oval — often with one end bigger than the other. Not all bird eggs have a big end and a small end. Owls and pigeons lay eggs with ends that are equal.

Birds lay relatively large eggs. A chicken lays an egg that weighs about one-thirtieth of its own body weight. If an egg of this weight were round, like a ball, it might stretch the oviduct and be painful to lay. An oval egg passes down the oviduct lengthwise without painfully stretching

Right: Birds called lapwings usually lay four eggs. The mother bird arranges the eggs, small end inward, so they fit neatly into the nest.

6

A red-eared terrapin's egg has a long oval shape.

An oystercatcher's egg is **camouflaged** in the wild.

Leaf-insect eggs do not look like eggs at all.

A brown argus butterfly egg looks like a patterned button.

Mosquito eggs are pointed and stick together. They float on water.

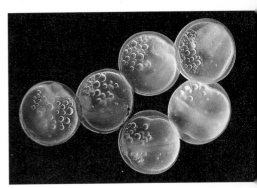

Stickleback eggs are clear and round.

the oviduct. Oval-shaped eggs also allow baby birds to develop inside the egg without cramping their bodies too much.

Fish eggs are usually round, or **spherical**, from whichever angle they are viewed. Fish can comfortably lay spherical eggs because the eggs are generally very small compared to the size of the female fish that lays them.

Insect eggs vary in shape from sharply pointed to button-shaped. Butterfly eggs are often beautifully patterned with ridges, dimples, or grooves.

Below: Trout eggs look like golden beads.

The Parts of an Egg

Top: A rainbow trout's egg has a tough skin. The food store consists of orange oil globules floating in clear liquid.

Eggs of all kinds are made of three distinct and vital parts. The shell protects the egg from the outside world. It may be brittle or leathery, but it allows air to pass through to the developing **embryo**. The **food store** is what the embryo uses to grow. A food store contains protein, oil, and enough water to keep the embryo moist. The tiny **nucleus** contains all the information necessary for the egg to develop into an animal of the same species that laid the egg.

Not only does the information in the nucleus determine what sort of animal hatches from the egg, but it also determines how the **hatchling** behaves. A baby bird, such as a pheasant or duckling, only hours old, knows to follow its

Below: The shell of a game pheasant's egg is hard and brittle.

Below: The shell of an orange-tip butterfly's egg is thin and clear. The food store inside is yellow.

Left: Baby mute swans hatch from their eggs already knowing they must follow their mother.

A scrub robin (above) brings a caterpillar to his chicks. Baby red-backed scrub robins (below) hatch from their eggs knowing how to open their mouths for food.

mother because this information was stored in the nucleus from which it developed.

The information in the nucleus of an egg is in the form of very complex **molecules** called **genes**. An egg nucleus contains many thousands of different genes that control the way the embryo develops. The egg starts off as a single **cell** but divides into millions of cells to form the embryo. Each new cell has its own nucleus that carries exactly the same combination of genes as was carried in the nucleus of the original egg cell. The cells of an embryo contain the same genes, but groups of cells grow in different ways to form different parts of the body.

Fertilizing the Egg

Below: A male common frog **(also pictured at top)** clutches a female. While the female was laying her eggs, the male released sperm into the water to fertilize the eggs.

All bird eggs and many other eggs will only develop if they have been **fertilized**. Eggs produced by a female are fertilized by tiny **sperm** from a male. Each sperm has its own nucleus and genes, just like the nucleus in an egg. Sperm are usually put inside the female's body by the male when animals **mate**, but many water-living animals do not mate. Eggs can be fertilized inside or outside the female's body. To fertilize fish and frog eggs, the male releases sperm into the water while the female lays her eggs. Sperm have long tails with which they can swim like tadpoles. They swim in search of an egg to fertilize.

Above: An African fish called a mouthbrooder laid her eggs on a flat rock. She picks them up in her mouth for safekeeping.

The male mouthbrooder has egg-like markings on his lower fin. He spreads his fin so that the female sees the fake eggs.

The female tries to pick up the fake eggs. The male releases sperm to fertilize the eggs held in her mouth.

A bird's egg is ready to be fertilized before its shell is formed. The egg has a soft skin. By swimming strongly against it, a sperm can get through. Once one sperm is inside the egg, no other sperm can enter. The nucleus of the sperm then joins up with the egg's nucleus. As a result, a fertilized egg contains genes from both parents.

Not all eggs need to be fertilized. For instance, ants, bees, and wasps lay both fertilized and unfertilized eggs. Fertilized eggs develop into females. Unfertilized eggs develop into males.

Left: A female red mason bee nests in a glass tube. She has built five pollen-filled compartments and laid an egg in each. The first two eggs are fertilized. The other three eggs are unfertilized.

11

Uncaring Egg-layers

If an animal lays only a few big eggs, each egg is important and needs to be looked after carefully.

When there are thousands of tiny eggs, the mother generally does not care for them. She may spread her eggs in many places. If only one egg in a thousand survives to grow into an adult, the mother will have at least left some offspring.

Fish that live in the open sea generally lay huge numbers of eggs. A female mackerel can lay half a million eggs at a time. When mackerel **spawn**, males and females gather together in **shoals** to release sperm and eggs. Once this is done, they swim off, leaving the fertilized eggs to drift in the water and take their chances. Only a few mackerel eggs grow into adult fish.

Some species of coral spawn together on one night each year. They release their eggs and sperm into the water eight nights after a full moon. The next day, the sea appears milky for many miles (kilometers) around due to the millions of tiny eggs floating in it.

A few land animals scatter their eggs. For instance, a female marbled white butterfly seems to perch almost anywhere in her grassland home to lay an egg. The egg then just drops to the ground. The **larva**, or caterpillar, develops inside the egg.

When little marbled white caterpillars hatch, they eat their way out of the egg. They feed on grass in order to grow.

Marbled white caterpillars are not far from their first meal. Their mothers wisely place the eggs within easy reach of food.

Above: Starfish and mussels produce millions of eggs. Barnacles produce millions of larvae. The eggs and larvae drift away on ocean currents.

Caring for Eggs

Top: A queen wasp builds a paper nest for her eggs. She is curled around, guarding her first egg.

Above: A female spider spins a ball-shaped cocoon around her eggs. She will guard it until the spiderlings hatch.

Most insect mothers are careful about where they lay their eggs. They may spend hours choosing just the right spot. Because many butterfly and moth caterpillars will often eat the leaves of only one kind of plant, the female has first to search for that certain plant. She then lays her eggs on the plant in a place where she hopes they will not be found by egg-eaters or parasites. Once the eggs have been laid, however, female insects generally do not care for them.

Not all insects stop caring for their eggs once they are laid. A female parent bug stands guard over her **clutch** for many days until the eggs hatch. Even then, she goes on caring for her

Right: A female parent bug shields her newly hatched babies from a hungry spider.

14

Left: A female leather-back turtle buries her eggs at the top of a sandy beach. She scuffs sand over the nest to hide it.

family, leading them to places where they can find food. Bees and wasps also take very good care of their eggs. They build nests in which the eggs are laid. After the larvae hatch, the adults also provide food for them.

Choosing the right spot for egg-laying is also vital for snakes, lizards, and turtles. Their eggs have to be kept moist and at the right temperature in order to hatch. A mother turtle selects a spot high on a sandy beach where she carefully buries her eggs. Sun on the sand above the eggs keeps them warm. Water below the eggs keeps them moist. The temperature at which the eggs are kept determines the sex of the baby turtles. Below a certain temperature, only males hatch. Above a slightly higher temperature, only females hatch.

Below: A female grass snake watches over her eggs in a moist compost heap. The rotting plant material warms the eggs.

Above: Gentoo penguins lay two eggs in a nest built of stones. The adults guard the eggs carefully.

Birds lay fewer and larger eggs than most other animals. Birds also take especially good care of their eggs. Because birds are **warm-blooded**, their eggs need to be **incubated**. The eggs have to be kept steadily at about the body temperature of the adult bird, until they hatch. Almost all birds incubate their eggs by sitting on them. Many birds develop a warm, featherless patch of skin on their undersides called a **brood patch** specifically for incubating. Sometimes only the female sits on the eggs, but the parents often take turns. The eggs of a small bird, like a swallow, may take only sixteen days to hatch, but eagle eggs can take five weeks.

Bird eggs also have to be turned regularly. If an egg is not turned, the developing chick sticks to the inside of the eggshell and cannot hatch. A parent bird turns all of the eggs with its beak every few hours.

Right: A female greater flamingo watches closely while her chick struggles out of its eggshell.

16

Left: European birds called long-tailed tits lay their eggs in a nest built of moss, lichen, and spiders' webs, lined with feathers. Here, the male brings home some web for the nest.

An important part of caring for eggs is nest-building. Many birds build elaborate nests in which to lay their eggs. A pair of long-tailed tits may spend two weeks collecting pieces of moss and lichen. They join these materials together with spiders' webs to form a domed structure with a hole in one side. The nest is lined with several hundred small feathers to keep the chicks warm when they hatch. The adults build the nest deep in a bush to be well hidden from **predators**.

Below: A female shag sits on her eggs in a nest of sticks.

Every so often, she turns the eggs with her beak.

Eggs Are Alive

A freshly laid chicken's egg is a simple, oval object. Inside there is some clear, slimy liquid called **albumen** plus a round blob of thick, yellow or orange liquid called the **yolk**. It is hard to believe that these substances are alive and will soon transform into a fluffy, cheeping chick.

A fertilized egg that is incubated starts to develop immediately. The nucleus, which is on the outside of the yolk, divides in two. Each new nucleus is inside its own cell and has a full set of genes from both father and mother. In about twenty minutes, both cells divide again, and then again, and the process continues until a tiny

Below: After one day of incubation, the embryo of a chicken's egg is a flat plate of cells on top of a yolk.

After two days, the embryo has a tiny heart and is surrounded by a ring of blood vessels.

After three days, the embryo has the beginnings of a backbone, and the heart beats strongly.

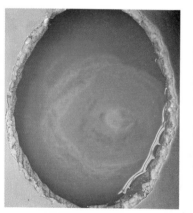
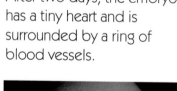
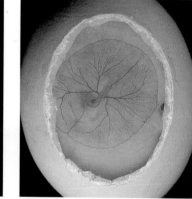

embryo is visible inside a ring of **blood vessels**. The blood vessels bring food from the albumen and the yolk so that the embryo can grow.

As the embryo grows, the blood vessels extend to the skin-like **membranes** just inside the eggshell. There, air is drawn in and carbon dioxide passes out through pores in the shell. The embryo breathes through the **porous** shell of its egg.

One of the first visible parts of a developing chick embryo is its heart. The heart starts to beat strongly after about three days of incubation. The flow of blood around the inside of the eggshell and through the embryo keeps it alive and healthy. The beating heart can sometimes be seen inside a pale-colored egg when it is examined under a bright light.

Above: Shining a bright light through a living pigeon egg — at fourteen days old — reveals a mass of red blood vessels. The dark spot is one of the embryo's eyes. The white area is the air space.

At seven days, the embryo has eyes, a brain, and tiny buds where limbs will develop.

At fourteen days, the chick embryo has a head and eyes, with much smaller feet and wings.

At twenty days, the chick is fully formed. But it has not yet used up all its yolk.

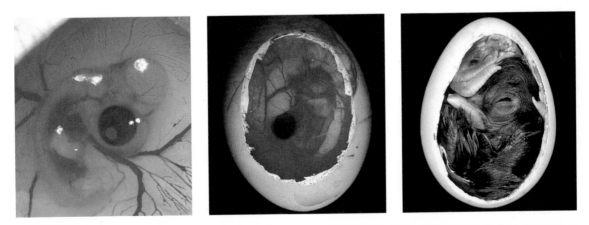

Above: A female common frog is shown with her spawn.

Not all eggs are like bird eggs. The eggs of frogs and newts have no shell. They are laid in water, and there is no risk that they will dry up. The black blobs in frogs' spawn are the egg cells. They can be clearly seen through the jelly. Unlike a bird's egg where cells form on the outside of the yolk, the entire egg cell of a frog's egg divides. At the first division, it is as if an invisible thread has been pulled tightly around the egg. Little folds appear as the cell is slowly cut in half. The second division cuts across the first, making four quarters. Divisions continue until the developing embryo is a hollow sphere built of cells.

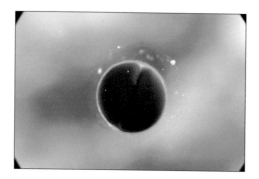

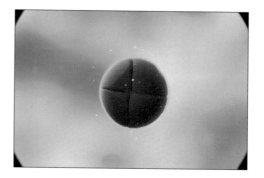

1. A frog egg divides in two soon after it has been laid.

2. After an hour or two, the egg divides again, making four cells.

3. In a few days, the egg consists of many cells.

4. In two to three weeks, the frog egg becomes a tadpole.

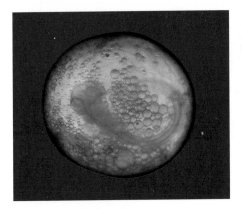

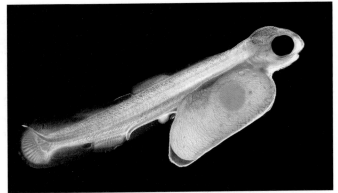

Above: The ghost-like shape of a baby trout can be seen developing inside this egg.

When the baby trout hatches, it carries with it a big sac of yolk.

Fish eggs are usually surrounded by a tough skin. Inside, there is not a clear distinction between albumen and yolk. Instead, there are globules of oil floating in watery liquid. These substances transform into a backbone with eyes and then gradually into a little fish.

The secret of an egg's development is in its genes. Genes are made of a nucleic acid called DNA. DNA molecules inside the egg control how the simple food store becomes an active animal. The animal is perfectly shaped and may even know how to feed itself and avoid danger.

Below: Once young trout have used up their yolk, they start to feed and grow quickly.

Hatching

Breaking out of an egg is a big effort for a baby bird. The shell is hard, and there are tough membranes inside the shell. Before the chick starts to hatch, it pushes its beak through the membranes into the air space inside the egg. The air space had been slowly increasing in size while the embryo developed to occupy about one-seventh of the egg. With the tip of its beak in the air space, the chick takes its first breath.

The next big effort for the chick is to crack the shell. It does this by placing the tip of its beak against the inside of the shell. Eggshell is strong when pressed from the outside, but it cracks much more easily when pressed from the inside. To crack the shell, the chick uses a little point on the tip of its beak called an egg tooth. Once the first crack, or **pip**, is made, fresh air rushes in. Then the chick may rest for several hours, doing nothing except breathing.

Having gained strength, the chick twists itself around very slightly. It makes another pip next to the first. Gradually, the chick makes a row of pips around the bigger end of the egg. When the row is about three-quarters of the way around, the chick gives a big heave, and the top of the egg pops off. Wet and kicking, the chick falls into the world outside the egg.

Left: A partridge chick breathes fresh air. Its egg tooth is visible on the tip of its beak.

Above: The partridge chick has cut the top off its egg with a row of pips and is pushing its way out.

Above: Once free of the egg, the little partridge will soon turn the right way up, dry out, and start running around.

Opposite: A baby moorhen has just cracked the top off its egg and hatched.

Right: A baby tortoise walks out of its round egg. It is hungry and tries to eat the shell.

The stages at which animals hatch from their eggs are very different. Some hatchlings look like small versions of their parents. They can walk or crawl away from their eggshells and start life on their own right away. Other hatchlings are completely helpless and, for a time, depend on their parents for all their needs.

Even very similar eggs may hatch at different stages. For instance, frogs that breed in water hatch into tadpoles. Other frogs that do not breed in water go through the tadpole stage in the egg. They hatch as fully formed froglets.

Similarly, the eggs of many sea snails hatch into tiny larvae that do not look at all like snails.

Right: With its sharp egg tooth, this baby rat snake has sliced through a tough eggshell. The baby blows bubbles as it hatches.

24

Left: When baby Roman snails are ready to hatch, they produce a liquid that dissolves most of the eggshell.

They swim around for some time before they become snails. Land snails also have larvae, but they do their swimming while still in the egg. They swim around and around inside the egg until they grow into little snails with shells. Only then is it safe for them to hatch.

Baby animals use many different ways to get free of their eggs. Snakes slice their way through their tough eggshells with a sharp egg tooth. Caterpillars eat their way out of their delicate, clear eggs. Once they are out, they turn around and eat the rest of the shell. Land snails produce a liquid that dissolves their chalky eggshells, leaving very little behind when they crawl away.

Above: A leaf insect egg has a ready-made lid. The baby insect pushes the lid off and climbs out.

Left: The caterpillar of an owl butterfly bites at the inside of its egg until there is a lid that it can push open.

After the Egg

Below: Fully formed baby aphids are laid by the mother **(top)**.

Bird eggs are laid, one at a time, as soon as each egg forms inside the female's body. It is important for birds to release their eggs quickly because they need to keep their bodies light enough to fly. For land creatures, however, extra weight is not such a problem. Many land animals carry a full clutch of eggs before laying them all at once.

Many snakes and lizards keep their eggs inside their bodies while the embryos are developing. This protects the eggs from egg-eaters and saves the female from producing eggshells. These internal eggs have thin skins. The young reptiles burst out of their eggs while still inside their mother. They are born ready to crawl away and look after themselves.

Below: The eggs of a swordtail fish hatch inside the female's body, and she gives birth to live fish. This baby is being born head first.

The mother swordtail fish jerks away as she gives birth. The babies are able to swim as soon as they are born.

26

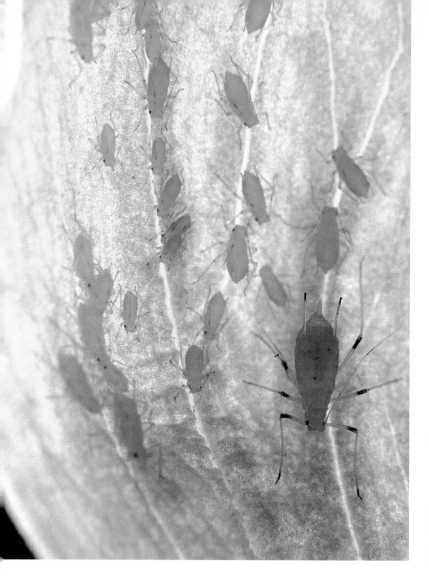

Left: A mother aphid feeds underneath a leaf, surrounded by her family of babies.

Below: A single tsetse fly egg hatches inside the female's body and grows there to a full-sized larva. The female lays the enormous larva that weighs more than herself.

Many fish, and even insects, such as aphids, have also given up egg-laying to produce fully formed young. But eggs are still the starting point for most animals.

An egg is a surprise package. It is smooth and rounded on the outside and liquid inside. It appears simple but is very complex.

If it is kept warm, the oval egg is like a clock with a timer that ticks away for many days. Then, just at the right moment, it cracks open, and a wriggling, kicking baby animal bursts out.

Activities:

Experiments with Eggs

Just about everyone knows what a chicken's egg looks and feels like and what it tastes like when cooked.

An egg breaks easily, but the thin shell is a lot stronger than you might think. Hold a hard-boiled egg between both your hands, with fingers interlocked (*as pictured*), so the

ends of the egg are resting in your palms. Now squeeze the egg, end-to-end between your hands, as hard as you can. If it breaks, either you are very strong or the egg is a weak one! Most eggs can withstand being squeezed in this way by a strong man.

If a strong man cannot break an egg, how can a little chick crack it? The answer lies both in the shape of the egg and in the nature of eggshell.

Eggshell is brittle and has very little strength if it is twisted or pulled apart. If it is pressed together, however, eggshell is very strong. The gentle curving shape of an egg means that, if it is pressed end-to-end, the shell is neither twisted nor pulled but is pressed together all over the egg.

Spinning eggs

Now spin a hard-boiled egg. A fast spin of the egg on a smooth surface will cause the egg to stand up on its end and remain there for several seconds.

Try doing the same with a raw egg. It is impossible. The liquid contents of the raw egg put the brakes on to prevent the egg from spinning. Cooking changes the nature of the proteins in the egg, causing them to become solid. Now you know how to tell the difference between a boiled egg and a raw one without having to crack them.

Hatching eggs

One of the most exciting things to do with eggs is to keep them in an incubator until they hatch. An incubator is a special box in which there is a heater that keeps the inside of the box at just the right temperature. All incubators have a place containing water so that the eggs are kept moist. Some incubators also have levers or rollers that will turn the eggs regularly.

Try hatching some eggs using an incubator that may be available at your school. Supermarket eggs will never hatch because the hens that lay them are kept without roosters, so the eggs are not fertilized. Have your teacher or another adult help you obtain chickens' or ducks' eggs from a farm or hatchery to be sure that they have been fertilized.

If the eggs are dirty, wipe them carefully with a damp cloth but do not put them in water. When the temperature of the incubator has been steady at about 99° Fahrenheit (37° Centigrade) for a day or so, put all the eggs in.

NOTE: *Have a teacher or another adult help you with this project.*

If your incubator does not have a turning device, you will have to turn the eggs by hand. Use a pencil to mark each egg with an X on one side and an O on the other.

Lay the eggs in the incubator so that all the Xs are up. When you turn the eggs, turn each halfway around so that all the Os are up. To be sure the embryos do not stick to the inside of their eggshells, you must turn the eggs at least twice a day — Os up at the first turn, Xs up at the second turn, and so on.

It is very important to follow the instructions on the incubator regarding adding water. Eggs that are too moist or too dry will not hatch properly. Watching the embryos develop is miraculous. After the eggs have been in the incubator for four days, take them out one by one, being careful not to let any of them get cool. In a darkened room, hold a flashlight under each egg. If the eggs are developing, you should be able to see a faint red blob surrounded by spidery blood vessels *(see page 19)*.

At a later time, you will be able to see the embryos twisting and turning as they exercise their new muscles. As the chicks grow inside their eggs, it becomes more and more difficult to see what is happening inside the egg. Eventually, only the air space can be seen — the rest of the egg does not let any light through.

The first pip should appear in chickens' eggs after twenty days in the incubator. Ducks' eggs take a week longer. Hatching can take as long as twenty-four hours, so do not feel tempted to help a chick that has been in a pipped egg for hours. If you try to help, you will probably damage blood vessels in the membranes and cause bleeding. Newly hatched chicks must be kept warm at all times. Have suitable food and water ready for them. When they become strong and active, return them to the farm or hatchery where you got the eggs.

Glossary

albumen: a mixture of proteins that form the "white" of an egg.

blood vessels: the tubes that carry blood throughout the body of an animal.

brood patch: a featherless patch on a bird's underside used to incubate eggs.

camouflaged: hidden from view due to special colors or patterns that cause an object to blend in with its surroundings.

cells: the microscopic building blocks of plant and animal bodies.

clutch: the full number of eggs laid by one bird or another egg-laying animal.

conundrum: a riddle or puzzling question.

embryo: an early stage in the development of an animal that takes place within the egg or in the female's body. An early stage of plants when they are within seeds is also called the embryo.

evolved: modified or changed slowly and gradually over time.

fertilized: joined with a sperm so that development can start. Most eggs will not develop unless they are fertilized.

food store: the part of an egg that provides nutrition for the embryo to grow.

genes: the very complex molecules that determine what characters are passed on from one generation to the next. There are thousands of genes in a cell, and every cell in an animal or plant contains the same set of genes.

hatchling: a baby animal that has just hatched from its egg.

incubated: kept warm.

larva: the early form of an animal.

mate (v): to join together (animals) to produce young.

membranes: several layers of thin, skin-like material.

molecules: the smallest parts of a substance, made up of two or more atoms joined together.

nucleus: the microscopic round object inside cells that contains genes.

oviduct: the tube in a female animal's body through which eggs pass.

pip: a small break in the shell of an egg made by a hatching chick.

porous: full of tiny holes through which gas or liquid can pass.

predator: an animal that hunts other animals for food.

reproduced: produced offspring.

shoal: a large group or number, such as a large group of fish.

spawn: to lay eggs in water. Fish, frogs, and toads spawn.

sperm: special male cells, usually actively swimming, that fertilize female egg cells. The word *sperm* can be singular or plural.

spherical: shaped like a ball.

warm-blooded: having blood that stays about the same temperature regardless of the surrounding air or water temperature.

yolk: the central food store in an egg.

Plants and Animals

The common names of plants and animals vary from language to language. But plants and animals also have scientific names, based on Greek or Latin words, that are the same the world over. Each plant and animal has two scientific names. The first name is called the genus. It starts with a capital letter. The second name is the species name. It starts with a small letter.

African mouthbrooder (*Haplochromys burtoni*) — Africa 11

chicken (*Gallus gallus*) — domesticated worldwide 4, 5, 18, 19, 28, 29

common frog (*Rana temporaria*) — Europe 10, 20

Gentoo penguin (*Pygoscelis papua*) — Antarctica 16

greater flamingo (*Phoenicopterus ruber*) — Africa, India, Southern Europe 16

leatherback turtle (*Dermochelys coriacea*) — oceans worldwide 15

long-tailed tit (*Aegithalos caudatus*) — Europe, Asia 17

marbled white butterfly (*Melanargia galathea*) — Europe 12

moorhen (*Gallinula chloropus*) — Europe, Asia, Africa 22-23

mute swan (*Cygnus olor*) — Europe, Asia, North America 9

ochre starfish (*Pisaster ochraceus*) — Northern Pacific coasts 13

orange-tip butterfly (*Anthocharis cardamines*) — Europe 8

owl butterfly (*Caligo* species) — South America 25

Pacific herring (*Clupea pallasi*) — Northern Pacific 12

red-backed scrub robin (*Erythropygia leucophrys*) — Africa 9

red-eared terrapin (*Pseudemys scripta*) — North America 7

red-legged partridge (*Alectoris rufa*) — Europe, introduced elsewhere 23

shag (*Phalacocorax aristotelis*) — North Atlantic coasts 17

spur-thighed tortoise (*Testudo graeca*) southern Europe 2, 24

swordtail (*Xiphophorus helleri*) — Central America 26

Texas rat snake (*Elaphe obsoleta*) — North America 24

three-spined stickleback (*Gasterosteus aculeatus*) — Europe, North America 7

Books to Read

The Amazing Egg Book. Margaret Griffin and Deborah Seed (Addison-Wesley)

Birds, Nests, and Eggs. Young Naturalist Field Guides (series). Mel Boring (Gareth Stevens)

Chicken and Egg. C. Back (Silver Burdett)

Dinosaur Eggs and Babies. Kenneth Carpenter (Cambridge University Press)

Owl Magic for Kids. Animal Magic (series). Neal D. Niemuth (Gareth Stevens)

What Hatches From An Egg? Leonardo Binato (Thomasson-Grant)

Videos and Web Sites

Videos

An Egg Becomes a Chick. (Coronet)
Egg Production. (Creative Educational Video)
Eggs to Market. (Phoenix/BFA)
Exploring the World of Birds. (Library Video)
The World of Baby Animals. (Questar, Inc)

Web Sites

www.nationalgeographic.com/features/96/ dinoeggs/
www/siec.K12.in.us/~west/strange/emu.htm
www.ahsc.arizona.edu/uac/iacuc/poultry/ species.shtml
kicon.com/stories/hundredeggs/e10.html
mstott.home.ml.org/

Some web sites stay current longer than others. For further web sites, use your search engines to locate the following topics: *birds, chickens, dinosaurs, eggs, fish, frogs, nests,* and *poultry.*

Index